THE BLACK DAHLIA
SHATTERED DREAMS

true crime

THE BLACK DAHLIA
SHATTERED DREAMS

by Brenda Haugen

Content Adviser: Philip Edney, Public Affairs Specialist,
Federal Bureau of Investigation, Washington, D.C.

Reading Adviser: Alexa L. Sandmann, EdD, Professor of
Literacy, College and Graduate School of Education,
Health, and Human Services, Kent State University

COMPASS POINT BOOKS
a capstone imprint

Compass Point Books
151 Good Counsel Drive
P.O. Box 669
Mankato, MN 56002-0669

Copyright © 2011 by Compass Point Books, a Capstone imprint.
All rights reserved. No part of this book may be reproduced
without written permission from the publisher. The publisher takes
no responsibility for the use of any of the materials or methods
described in this book, nor for the products thereof. Printed in the
United States of America in North Mankato, Minnesota.
032010   005740CGF10

 This book was manufactured with paper containing
at least 10 percent post-consumer waste.

Editor: Angie Kaelberer
Designers: Tracy Davies and Gene Bentdahl
Media Researcher: Marcie Spence
Library Consultant: Kathleen Baxter
Production Specialist: Jane Klenk

Library of Congress Cataloging-in-Publication Data
Haugen, Brenda.
  The Black Dahlia : shattered dreams / by Brenda Haugen.
      p. cm. — (True crime)
  Includes bibliographical references and index.
  ISBN 978-0-7565-4358-7 (library binding)
 1. Short, Elizabeth, 1924–1947. 2. Murder—California—Los
Angeles—Juvenile literature. 3. Murder—Investigation—
California—Los Angeles—Juvenile literature. I. Title. II. Series.
  HV6534.L7H39 2011
  364.152'3092—dc22   2010011206

Image Credits: AP Images, cover (top and bottom right), 21,
42, 83, Ric Francis, 87; Bettmann/Corbis, 76; FBI/AP Images,
27; International News Photo/AFP/Getty Images Inc., 13, 33;
International News Photo/Getty Images Inc., 10, 17, 50, 55, 67;
iStockphoto/Lobsterclaws, cover (bottom far right), MarsBars,
cover (middle), RBFried, cover (bottom left); Paramount Pictures/
Getty Images Inc., 36; Shutterstock/JoLin (cracked glass design used
throughout) Tania Zbrodko, 2; TMS/AP Images, 64

Visit Compass Point Books on the Internet at *www.capstonepub.com*

IN DEATH BETTY ACHIEVED THE FAME SHE DESIRED MOST OF HER LIFE.

Few crimes are so shocking or so terrifying that the stories of what happened live on years, or even decades, after the offenses occurred. The shock waves from these crimes often ripple beyond the areas where they happened, fascinating and frightening entire nations—and sometimes the world. Some of these crimes are solved. Often they are not. But even when the cases grow cold, the evidence remains and awakens the amateur detective in all of us.

TABLE OF CONTENTS

8	The Worst News Possible
14	Dreaming of a Better Life
24	Dashed Hopes
30	A Dangerous Path
40	Running Away
48	A Gruesome Discovery
62	True Confession?
72	Many Suspects
82	Continued Interest
88	Timeline
92	Glossary
93	Additional Resources
94	Select Bibliography
96	Index

CHAPTER 1

THE WORST NEWS POSSIBLE

Tricking a person to get information isn't something most people think is acceptable. Still, as newspaper reporter Wain Sutton dialed the telephone on January 16, 1947, he knew that was what he had to do. His boss, James Richardson, was listening in on the call. With five daily newspapers in Los Angeles, California, reporters competed fiercely for scoops that would make readers buy their papers.

"Hello. Mrs. Phoebe Short?" Sutton asked nervously. "Eh ... Mrs. Short, this is Wain Sutton of the *Los Angeles Examiner*."

As Richardson urged him on, Sutton told Phoebe the story his boss had invented. Sutton informed Phoebe that her daughter Elizabeth had won a beauty contest in Santa Barbara, California. Phoebe's voice bubbled with excitement, but she wasn't entirely surprised by the news. Her daughter was a dark-haired, blue-eyed beauty who was full of confidence and charm. She had won beauty contests before, including one in her hometown of Medford, Massachusetts, where Phoebe still lived.

Elizabeth "Betty" Short's striking looks won her several beauty contests.

As Phoebe spoke proudly about her daughter, whom she called Betty, Sutton gave Richardson an angry look. Phoebe was so happy about the news. As she talked about a letter she'd recently received from Betty, Sutton continued to let her believe the lie. He asked where the letter came from, and Phoebe gave him a return address in San Diego, California.

"It had been written while visiting friends in San Diego," Phoebe said of the January 8, 1947, letter. She went on to tell Sutton that Betty planned to return to Los Angeles with a man she called Red.

Richardson signaled to Sutton that he could now tell Phoebe the horrible truth. Sutton told Phoebe that he wasn't calling because Betty had won a beauty contest. He was calling because the 22-year-old had been brutally murdered. The day before, police had found Betty's mutilated body dumped in the Leimert Park neighborhood of Los Angeles.

THE BODY POLICE HAD FOUND COULDN'T BE THAT OF HER BELOVED DAUGHTER.

Phoebe was stunned. At first she said there had to be some sort of mistake. The body police had found couldn't be that of her beloved daughter. Slowly she came to realize that Sutton was telling the truth. Now she was the one who wanted answers. She demanded to know what had happened.

Sutton told Phoebe that his newspaper would pay her airfare and find a place for her to stay if she would come for the inquest, which was set for January 22 in Los Angeles. Hoping she could help with the investigation, Phoebe accepted the offer. She didn't know that Richardson had agreed to make the offer in an effort to keep her away from police and other newspapers' reporters. He wanted to get as much information from her as he could before anyone else could get to her.

While they waited for Phoebe to come to Los Angeles, the reporters had plenty of work to do. They now had an address in San Diego to investigate. Did the person or people living at the address know what happened to Betty? Who was this guy Betty had called Red? Could he be her killer?

Betty (right) was raised by her mother, Phoebe Short.

CHAPTER 2

DREAMING OF A BETTER LIFE

Betty Short had gone to California to seek fame and fortune. She also hoped to find a husband and have the happy life that had escaped her as a child.

Betty was born July 29, 1924, in Hyde Park, Massachusetts. She was the third of five girls born to Cleo and Phoebe Short. Cleo, a veteran of World War I, prospered as an auto mechanic, opening his own garage after his return from battle. Along with raising their family, Phoebe helped Cleo's business by attending to the bookkeeping and billing.

Their business soon took a new direction, however. In the 1920s miniature golf courses were growing more popular. Cleo began building miniature golf courses in the Boston, Massachusetts, area, and he moved his family to nearby Medford.

But in 1929 the stock market crash—and the Great Depression that followed—hit the Short family hard. People were struggling to put food on their families' tables. They didn't have money to spend on playing games of miniature golf. Soon Cleo's company had no work, and the bank foreclosed on it.

DARK DAYS

The Great Depression was a worldwide economic depression that started with the U.S. stock market crash October 29, 1929. When the stock market crashed, thousands of Americans lost large amounts of money. People stopped buying products and services and tried to save their money instead. With fewer people buying their products, many factories closed. The people who worked there lost their jobs. Without jobs, workers could no longer pay back loans, which caused banks to fail. When the banks closed, customers lost the money in their accounts. The Depression lasted until factories started producing weapons and other materials for World War II, which the United States entered in December 1941.

Betty dreamed of a career in the movie business.

Cleo vanished one day in 1930. Police found his car parked on the Charlestown Bridge in Boston. Police didn't find his body, but they figured Cleo had jumped from the bridge and drowned in the Charles River.

Phoebe had little time to mourn her husband. She had five children to support. She worked as a bookkeeper when she could, but steady jobs were hard to find. The family often had to rely on government handouts.

With her meager income, Phoebe could not pay the rent on her large home. She eventually moved with the girls to a two-bedroom house in Medford. Though the house was small, Phoebe made sure it was in a good neighborhood, where she and her daughters would be safe.

Phoebe also tried to make sure her daughters found some joy in life. Two or three times a week she took Betty and her sister Muriel to the movies.

"My other sisters weren't interested in the movies unless they were on dates," Muriel said. "I don't know why Betty and I were like Mama. ... We loved the movies!"

Phoebe, Betty, and Muriel made an event of the movie outings. They'd dress up and leave the house early to window-shop. Though they usually couldn't afford to buy what they looked at, Phoebe encouraged her daughters to dream of better futures. Betty didn't need much encouragement to dream. She talked about moving to Hollywood and becoming a famous actress.

Betty was plagued with health problems, including asthma. Sometimes the asthma attacks were so severe that Phoebe had to call a doctor in the middle of the night. He'd give Betty an adrenaline shot to help her breathe.

In 1939 15-year-old Betty underwent surgery to help clear her lungs. The operation helped, but doctors told her mother that Medford's cold winters would continue to trouble Betty. They advised Phoebe to send Betty somewhere with a milder climate.

The next winter 16-year-old Betty went to stay with friends of Phoebe's in Miami Beach, Florida. Betty found a part-time job working at a beach resort. The mild Florida winters greatly helped Betty's health. She wrote to her family that she hadn't had an asthma attack since leaving home.

Betty dropped out of high school after her sophomore year. The next two winters, she returned to Florida. Each spring she'd go home to Medford. Her family and friends noticed changes in Betty. She was growing up. She started wearing heavy makeup. Though she was still a teenager, she looked older and more sophisticated. Men were starting to pay attention to her.

In 1942 the Short family got a shock. Phoebe received a letter from her husband, Cleo. For 12 years Phoebe and her daughters had believed that Cleo was dead. Cleo explained that he'd left because of his financial problems. He was living in Vallejo, California, and working at the Mare Island Naval Shipyard. Cleo asked Phoebe to forgive him for leaving. He wanted to go back home.

Betty (left), with her friend Marge Dyer, enjoyed Florida's warm weather during her winters there.

Phoebe had worked hard to keep her family together. She'd received no help from Cleo during the years he'd been gone. She angrily replied that she couldn't forgive him for what he'd done. She didn't want him back.

Betty reacted differently. She was thrilled to hear that her father was alive. Adding to her excitement was the fact that he was living in California. The warm weather there would be good for her health. Although Vallejo was still quite a

ALL SHE COULD TALK ABOUT WAS MOVING TO CALIFORNIA AND HER DREAMS OF A CAREER IN HOLLYWOOD.

distance from Hollywood—and Betty's dreams of becoming a movie star—it was closer than Medford.

Betty wrote to her father. She told him about her dream of moving to California. Cleo wrote back. He said he'd send her money for a train ticket. If she wanted to, she could live with him until she found a job and was able to live on her own. Betty jumped at the chance. All she could talk about was moving to California and her dreams of a career in Hollywood.

"I asked her if she was going to be a movie star," said Mary Hernon, a girl who lived next door to the Short family. "She laughed and told me that's what she hoped to do, and if you wanted to be a movie star, it wasn't going to happen to you in Medford. She'd have to go to Hollywood."

CHAPTER 3

DASHED HOPES

Betty happily left the cold of Boston on a train bound for sunny California in December 1942. Her excitement didn't last long, however.

Life with her father was difficult. Betty's beauty and friendly personality attracted many men. Cleo criticized her for going out too often and for dating sailors from nearby Mare Island. Cleo also expected Betty to keep his house clean, but she didn't even clean up after herself. Her untidiness, her dating habits, and her dreams of stardom caused many arguments between father and daughter. In late January 1943, Betty moved out. She headed south to Camp Cooke, an Army post near Lompoc, California. She got a job as a cashier at the post store.

Finding a place to live proved more difficult. Because there was a housing shortage on the post, Betty lived with friends. At one point a sergeant offered Betty a place to stay. She accepted the offer, believing that the sergeant understood she wasn't romantically interested in him. The sergeant,

SWEETHEART OF CAMP COOKE

Betty quickly became very popular with the young soldiers at Camp Cooke. She provided a welcome distraction for them as they waited to be shipped off to war. Though she wasn't at Camp Cooke long, she gained enough attention to be voted "Camp Cutie."

however, became angry when she rebuffed his advances. Betty said he threatened and beat her, and she had a black eye to prove it.

After living for a time with a Women's Army Auxiliary Corps sergeant, Betty left the camp. She stayed with a female friend who had an apartment in Santa Barbara, California. The friend lived with a male soldier, but she let Betty sleep on the couch. For a while, things were good. Then trouble found Betty again.

On September 23, 1943, Betty was at a restaurant with a group of girls and soldiers. They were drinking alcohol and getting loud. Police were called, and 19-year-old Betty was arrested for being underage in a business where liquor was served.

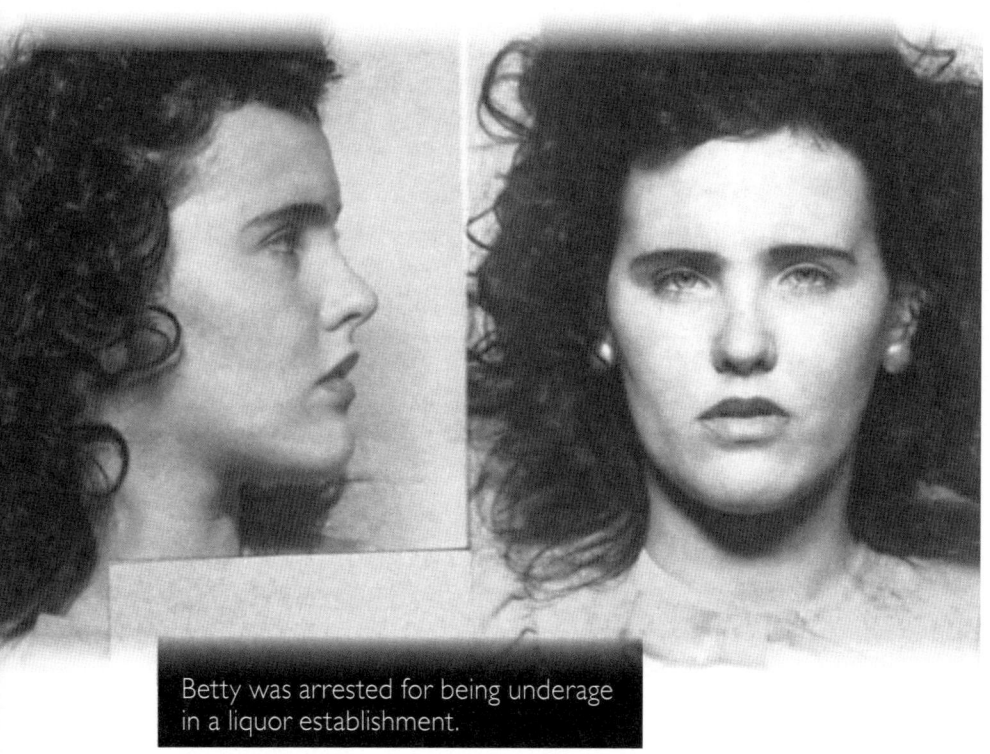

Betty was arrested for being underage in a liquor establishment.

At the police station, Betty was fingerprinted and had to pose for mug shots. The police wouldn't allow Betty to return to her apartment because her

UNKEFER TOLD BETTY TO STAY OUT OF TROUBLE.

true crime | 28 | DASHED HOPES

roommate lived with a soldier. At the time, people weren't considered adults until age 21. At 19, Betty was still a minor. She couldn't legally live at the apartment with the unmarried couple.

Police officer Mary Unkefer felt sorry for Betty. Unkefer allowed Betty to stay in her home until the police could figure out what to do with her. Cleo was contacted, but he didn't want Betty back. Eventually the police decided to send Betty home to her mother in Medford. Unkefer drove Betty to the bus station, gave her $10, and told her to stay out of trouble.

Betty would follow the officer's advice—at least for a while.

CHAPTER 4

A DANGEROUS PATH

Betty stayed with her family in Medford for several weeks before heading south to Miami, Florida, for the winter. She lived at a hotel and worked as a waitress. She told her family she was also doing some modeling.

Betty moved back to Los Angeles in August 1944. For a while she stayed downtown at the Clinton Hotel, which was operated by a man named Nate Bass. He had ties to organized crime and prostitution. Betty and her roommate, Lucille Varela, weren't prostitutes, but they were B-girls at Hollywood clubs. The clubs paid B-girls to flirt with male customers and encourage the men to keep buying drinks. The girls also tried to get some money for themselves. If a man got drunk and passed out, his wallet was easy pickings.

Most B-girls earned just enough to pay their living expenses. Young women like Betty and Lucille played the B-girl game to survive while they waited for their big breaks in show business.

One of Betty's favorite hangouts in 1944 was a club called the Hollywood Canteen. Servicemen gathered there. So did movie stars, who went there to raise the troops' spirits. Betty volunteered as a junior hostess at the club, dancing and flirting with the servicemen. She received free meals in return.

ANOTHER MURDERED GIRL

Georgette Bauerdorf started working at the Hollywood Canteen about the same time Betty did. On October 12, 1944, Georgette was murdered in her West Hollywood apartment. Her badly beaten body was found floating in her bathtub. A cloth had been shoved in her throat, and she had apparently choked on it. Several servicemen who knew Georgette from the Hollywood Canteen were considered suspects in the case, but no arrests were ever made. Georgette's murder remains unsolved.

Betty dated Major Matt Gordon in 1945.

Betty met Lieutenant Joseph Fickling at the Hollywood Canteen in September 1944. Fickling was a pilot stationed at Long Beach, California. They began dating, but it didn't last long. Fickling was soon shipped out to England.

That winter Betty moved back to Miami. She thought she'd found true love when she met U.S. Army Air Forces pilot Matt Gordon. She wrote to her mother and said he had asked her to marry him.

Whether Betty and Gordon became engaged remains a question. Some friends say they did. His family says they didn't. In any case, they exchanged many letters after he went overseas and she went home to Medford.

BETTY WAS HEARTBROKEN. GORDON'S DEATH SEEMED TO CHANGE HER.

But Gordon never returned to Betty. In November 1945 he died in a plane crash in India. Gordon's mother sent Betty a telegram with the news.

Betty was heartbroken. Gordon's death seemed to change her. She started wearing white powder on her face and bright red lipstick. With her dark hair, the look was quite dramatic and drew lots of attention, especially from men.

She also started contacting old friends. Among them was Lieutenant Fickling. He said he'd be coming back to the United States in June 1946 and would love to see her. They made plans to meet in Chicago, Illinois.

Fickling only had two days to spend in Chicago before he had to report to Long Beach. When he got to California, Fickling sent Betty money for a train ticket to join him.

But after Betty arrived in Long Beach, their relationship wasn't what she had expected. Fickling lived on the military post. Betty had to live miles away at a hotel. Fickling wanted to date Betty, but he didn't want to marry her.

About the same time Betty moved to Long Beach, a movie called *The Blue Dahlia* was released. Two of Betty's soldier friends jokingly called her the Black Dahlia because of her mane of dark hair and the fact she often wore form-fitting black clothes. The nickname stuck.

At the end of August, Fickling was discharged from military service. He moved to his parents' home in Charlotte, North Carolina. He'd never see Betty again.

Alan Ladd and Veronica Lake starred in *The Blue Dahlia*.

THE BLUE DAHLIA

The movie *The Blue Dahlia* boasted two of the biggest stars of the 1940s, Alan Ladd and Veronica Lake. The crime thriller, which was nominated for an Academy Award, told the story of a former bomber pilot who was suspected of murdering his unfaithful wife. The Blue Dahlia was a nightclub owned by the wife's boyfriend.

After her relationship with Fickling ended, Betty kept searching for her place in the world. Police would later discover that during a five-month period in 1946, she lived in at least 11 places in Los Angeles. She also dated many men.

Betty also had several female friends, but no one really knew her very well. Despite surrounding herself with people, she rarely talked about her private life. And when she did talk about it, she often wasn't truthful. According to police officer Vince Carter:

"Miss Short's life in Hollywood seemed to follow a pattern. She didn't have any visible signs of employment, she'd be broke, and then suddenly have some money. Her roommates, the bartenders, and the hotel clerks all came up with the same story. She was secretive—never one to confide. She never said what she was really doing, or who she was really going out with, or where she was really going.

"Several of Elizabeth's girlfriends ... said there were days when she would disappear. Each time she would be gone for a day or two after saying she was going to hitch a ride down to Sixth Street. Upon her return, she was always loaded with money and would pay all her bills. ... I believe there were some acquaintances who knew her tragic story ... but they were afraid to talk about it because it involved some powerful and dangerous people."

In early December 1946, Betty decided to leave Los Angeles. The night before she left, she told friends she was scared. Sherryl Maylond, her roommate at the Chancellor Apartments, knew that Betty had received several phone calls from Maurice Clement, a man who had connections to organized crime. Clement, who sometimes paid Betty's bills, was also known to be involved in prostitution. Had Betty become mixed up in it as well? Some people guessed that Betty may even have become pregnant and that Clement was trying to force her to have an abortion, which was illegal at the time. No one knew anything for sure. Though her friends realized that she was frightened, she kept the reason to herself.

Betty did tell Sherryl Maylond that she was going to Oakland, California, to visit her sister Virginia. Betty's sister said later that they'd made no such plans. Instead, on December 6, Betty went to San Diego, a city where she didn't know a soul.

CHAPTER 5

RUNNING AWAY

The last movie had ended, and usher Dorothy French was about to close the Aztec Theatre in San Diego the evening of December 8. As she was finishing her work, French noticed a young woman who had fallen asleep in one of the front rows.

The woman was Betty. She told French she had no money and nowhere to go. Betty said she had worked in a theater in Boston and wondered whether she could get a job at the Aztec.

French felt sorry for Betty. She invited her to spend the night in the home she shared with her mother and brother. Betty gladly accepted the offer.

Though it was late, Elvera French was still awake when her daughter arrived with Betty. French's mother welcomed the stranger and said Betty could sleep on the couch.

Elvera French told Betty that her husband had been killed in the war. Betty said she also had lost her husband in the war. She talked about Matt Gordon as if they had been married. Betty added

The black clothes Betty often wore led to her nickname, the Black Dahlia.

that she'd had a son with him, but that the baby had died at birth. This also was a lie. She had never been married or had a baby.

Betty promised the Frenches she wouldn't stay more than a couple of days. She also offered to pay them for their hospitality.

"I told her that was not necessary," Dorothy French said. "A lot of people were having a hard time—the housing and apartment shortage was bad, and my mother also told her not to worry about putting us out, and whatever she needed, we'd be able to take care of it."

Betty said she didn't want to inconvenience the Frenches or take advantage of their generosity. But her actions didn't match her words.

Though Betty said she'd be starting a new job soon, she never did. Instead she slept late every morning. It wasn't unusual for Betty to be found in her pajamas at 2:00 p.m. When Elvera French came home for lunch, she'd tiptoe around her own home because she didn't want to disturb her sleeping guest.

At night Betty stayed out late. After only a few days in San Diego, she already had a growing group of male admirers wanting to take her out on the town.

While staying with the Frenches, Betty wrote many letters, including one to her mother. It was the return address from one of these letters that Phoebe gave to newspaper reporter Wain Sutton.

On January 2, 1947, Betty wrote to her friend Ann Toth in Los Angeles, asking for money. A couple of days later, two men and a woman came to the French home looking for Betty.

"She [Betty] became very frightened—she seemed to get panicky, and didn't want to see the people or answer the door," Dorothy French said. "They finally went back to the car and drove away."

On January 8 Betty's friend Robert "Red" Manley stopped by. He was a traveling salesman from Los Angeles who had met Betty shortly after she arrived in San Diego. Though Manley was married, he was interested in Betty and called on her when he was in San Diego on business. Betty was happy to see Manley when he arrived at the French home, and she told him she needed to get back to Los Angeles.

"I'm leaving here," she said. "Maybe you can take me someplace to get a room for the night, and I can take a bus in the morning."

Betty left with Manley. The couple stopped at a restaurant to eat and then went to a couple of nightclubs. They spent the night in a motel. The next morning Manley had a business appointment. When he returned to the motel about 12:30 p.m., Betty was ready to leave. They drove back to Los Angeles. When they arrived Manley took Betty to the bus station, where she stored her luggage. The couple then drove to the Biltmore Hotel. Betty said she was going to meet her sister Virginia there.

WHETHER BETTY INTENDED TO MEET SOMEONE ELSE OR HAD OTHER PLANS THAT EVENING REMAINS A MYSTERY.

Manley hung around for a while, but Virginia never arrived. Virginia later said she and her sister hadn't planned to meet in Los Angeles. Whether Betty intended to meet someone else or had other plans that evening remains a mystery. Manley had to get home to his wife and son. He said goodbye to Betty about 6:30 p.m. and left her in the hotel lobby.

People at the hotel saw Betty use the lobby telephone several times after Manley left. If she had planned to meet someone there, he or she never showed up. Betty finally left the hotel at 10:00 p.m. It was the last time she was seen alive.

CHAPTER 6

A GRUESOME DISCOVERY

The chill in the air didn't make Bobby Jones' early-morning job any more pleasant.

Sunrise was a long way off when he got up January 15, 1947, to fold newspapers before delivering them on his route along Crenshaw Boulevard in Los Angeles. By about 4:00 a.m., Bobby was walking his bike through the tall weeds covering the empty lots of the Leimert Park neighborhood on the way to his route. Bobby heard a car behind him. He saw an older black sedan park by one of the empty lots. It was strange that the car didn't have its lights on. He glanced at the car's windshield, but he couldn't see anyone inside.

Bobby didn't have time to dwell on it. The bottoms of his pants legs were cold and damp from the dewy weeds. He wanted to get his papers delivered. He kept walking.

About six hours later, Betty Bersinger was pushing her 3-year-old daughter in a stroller near the vacant lots. As she walked toward a shoe repair shop a few blocks away, she noticed something

Betty's body was found in a vacant lot in the Leimert Park area of Los Angeles.

white lying in a vacant lot. At first it looked like an unclothed mannequin. It had been broken into two pieces at the waist. As Bersinger drew closer, she realized that the figure wasn't a mannequin. It was a naked woman.

Bersinger stopped at the first house she came to and knocked on the door. A woman answered the

A FRANTIC CALL

When Betty Bersinger called police after finding the body, she was so upset that she hung up the phone before leaving her name. Either she gave a limited description of what she'd found or the person taking her call at the police station misunderstood what Bersinger was saying. When the radio call went out to police officers, it was labeled "Code 2-390 W-415." Code 2 meant police should go to the scene as quickly as possible but not use their red lights or sirens. The 390 meant a drunk, and W stood for woman. The 415 meant indecent exposure.

door, and Bersinger told her about the body. The woman let Bersinger use the phone to call police.

Officers Will Fitzgerald and Frank Perkins were the first to respond to the call. They, like all other Los Angeles police officers, were used to dealing with grisly crimes. But even they were shocked by the gruesome scene. A woman's body lay on the grass near the sidewalk. Though the naked body was cut in two, there was no blood on it or in the grass. This led police to believe she had been killed somewhere else. The grass under the body was wet with dew. Police guessed that the victim had been dumped at the site after 2:00 a.m., when the temperature had dipped low enough for dew to form.

The woman's body also showed other injuries. Among them was a slash from each side of her mouth nearly to her ears. Rope marks on her wrists and ankles led police to believe she had been tied up.

When detectives Harry Hansen and Finis Brown arrived at the scene around noon, police, reporters, and curious onlookers were buzzing around the area. Hardened crime reporter Aggie Underwood of the *Los Angeles Herald-Express* turned pale when she first saw the body.

"You could see the color drain right out of her like you'd opened a spigot on her bottom side," one police officer said of Underwood's reaction.

Hansen worried that valuable evidence was being lost. Reporters had walked around the scene and dropped used camera flashbulbs and cigarette butts on the ground. Bystanders stood near the murder scene or on top of their cars to get a better look. The braver ones among the crowd had ventured onto the vacant lot. Hansen ordered uniformed officers to clear the crime scene.

Around 2:00 p.m. a hearse arrived to take the body to the Los Angeles County morgue. With no clue to the victim's identity, she was simply called "Jane Doe #1." Police knew finding out her real name wasn't going to be easy. Because she had been so disfigured, photos of the dead young woman weren't going to resemble what she had looked like when she was alive. An artist from the *Examiner* was allowed to make a sketch of the victim. Police hoped the sketch would lead someone to recognize and identify her.

The staff at the *Examiner* also volunteered to help get fingerprints taken from the victim identified. In the days before computers, fingerprints were examined at FBI headquarters in Washington, D.C. The Los Angeles crime lab mailed the fingerprint card of Jane Doe #1 to the FBI. Because Washington was in the midst of a winter storm, delivery of the card could be delayed for days. But the *Examiner* had a new Soundphoto machine, similar to today's fax machines, that sent photos instantly to other newspaper offices around the country. Though it had never been done before, the fingerprints could be sent to the FBI the same way.

At 4:00 a.m. on January 16, the police gave it a try. The first prints sent weren't detailed enough for the FBI to identify. So the *Examiner* photo lab staff enlarged the prints and sent them again.

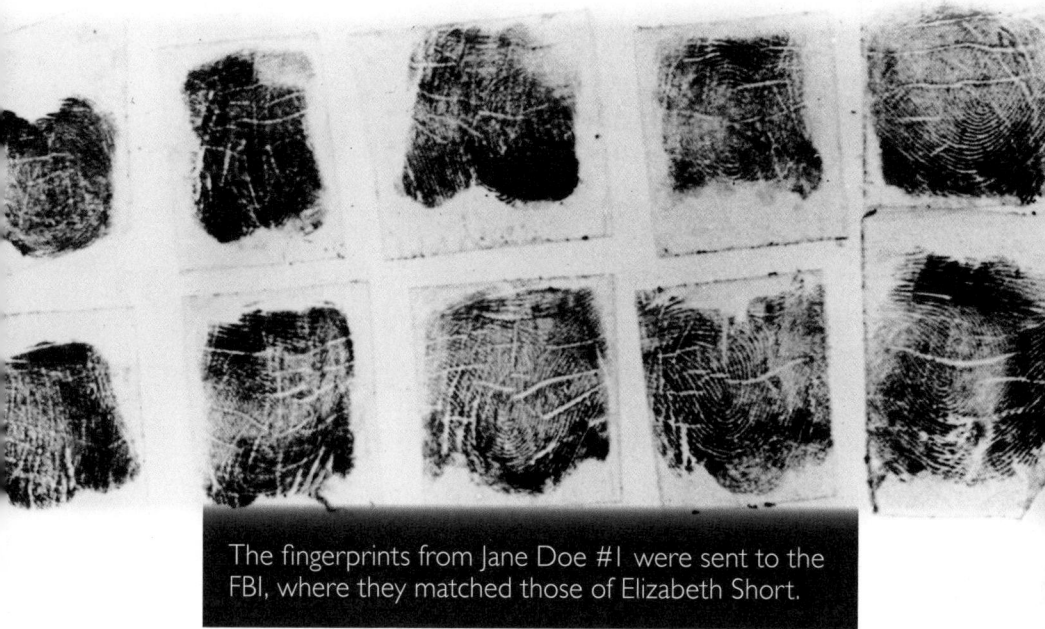

The fingerprints from Jane Doe #1 were sent to the FBI, where they matched those of Elizabeth Short.

In less than an hour, Jane Doe #1 was identified as Elizabeth Short. The FBI had been able to match the victim's fingerprints with the prints taken from Betty when she applied for a job at Camp Cooke and when she'd been arrested for underage drinking in 1943. The police had the victim's identity, and the *Examiner* reported the news first.

"This scoop put the *Examiner* so far ahead of its opposition, they were never able to catch up," said

> **"BLACK IS NIGHT, MYSTERIOUS, FORBIDDING EVEN; THE DAHLIA IS AN EXOTIC AND MYSTERIOUS FLOWER."**

Will Fowler, a reporter for the *Examiner*. "Hours before other papers had a clue that the body had ever been identified, our crew of reporters and photogs were digging into Elizabeth Short's life. The competition actually had to read our paper before they knew what step to take next in the investigation. [James] Richardson's crew worked so effectively with the clues we were digging up on our own that we were able to start making deals with [Los Angeles Police Department] Homicide."

But Aggie Underwood, the crime reporter at the *Herald-Express*, got at least one scoop of her own. She uncovered the fact that in the clubs of

Hollywood and Long Beach, Betty was known as the Black Dahlia.

"There were crimes that same year that were at least as heinous and victims at least as pretty and none of them got anywhere near the same attention," Detective Harry Hansen said later. "It was that name 'Black Dahlia' that set this one off … just those words strung together in that order turned Elizabeth Short's murder into a coast-to-coast sensation. Black is night, mysterious, forbidding even; the dahlia is an exotic and mysterious flower. There could not have been a more intriguing title. Any other name wouldn't have been anywhere near the same."

A few hours after Betty Short's fingerprints were identified, her body lay on a table in the Los Angeles County morgue. The strong smell of the formaldehyde used to preserve bodies from decay hung in the air. Chief Surgeon Frederick Newbarr joined Deputy Coroners Victor CeFalu and Louis Delgado. They would perform the autopsy on

Betty's body, trying to discover exactly when and how she died.

Before the autopsy CeFalu said Betty might have choked on the blood from the multiple cuts to her face. But Newbarr couldn't find any blood or other obstruction in her throat. He noted many cuts on several areas of the body. He examined her heart, lungs, and brain. At the end of the autopsy, he told police that Betty's death was caused by blows to her head and the shock of the blood loss from the cuts to her face. Her body had been cut in two after her death.

Newbarr also said he could find no evidence that Betty had been sexually assaulted. However, police were considering the murder a sex crime. The day Betty's body was discovered, police questioned more than 150 known sex offenders. Not one of them provided any useful information. Police also interviewed Elvera and Dorothy French about Betty's last days. The Frenches told police about Betty's relationship with a man named Bob. They said they didn't know Bob's last name, but they remembered that he drove a tan Studebaker coupe. A motel registry in Pacific Beach, California, described a car of that make that was owned by Robert "Red" Manley. He quickly became the number-one suspect.

Examiner reporter Will Fowler had a special badge from the Los Angeles County sheriff's office. He flashed the badge when Manley's wife, Harriet, opened her door to him January 18. Harriet Manley told Fowler that her husband was traveling with his boss, J.W. Palmer, and was expected home the next day. Manley had left his car at Palmer's home. Fowler gave this information to his boss, James Richardson, who in turn told the police. Detectives immediately set up a stakeout at Palmer's home. They weren't going to let Manley get away.

On the evening of January 19, police were waiting when Manley stepped out of Palmer's car in front of the Palmer house. Manley was walking toward the Studebaker parked in the driveway when the detectives jumped out of their car, guns drawn.

"I KNOW WHY YOU'RE HERE, BUT I DIDN'T DO IT."

true crime | 60 | A GRUESOME DISCOVERY

Manley held up his arms. "I know why you're here," he said, "but I didn't do it." The detectives quickly handcuffed him and took him to the Hollenbeck police station for questioning.

Through the night Detectives Hansen and Brown fired questions at Manley. They also gave him two lie detector tests, which he passed. He insisted he hadn't seen Betty after dropping her off at the Biltmore January 9 and that he had nothing to do with her murder. After hours of questioning, Manley finally collapsed. His nerves were shattered, and he was exhausted.

Detective Hansen eventually realized that Manley was telling the truth. After two days in jail, Manley was released. The police were right back where they started.

CHAPTER 7

TRUE CONFESSION?

The same day Will Fowler was interviewing Red Manley's wife, Phoebe Short arrived in Los Angeles. At the airport she spoke with reporters and a representative of the coroner's office. Phoebe then traveled north to Berkeley, California, to spend the days before the inquest with her daughter Virginia and Virginia's husband, Adrian West. They took an airplane to Los Angeles January 22. Reporters from the *Examiner* picked them up at the airport and drove them to the Hall of Justice. There, at the coroner's office, the family had to officially identify Betty's body.

Detectives Harry Hansen and Finis Brown led the women to a window between two rooms. On the other side of the glass was a sheet-draped body on a gurney. When the sheet was pulled back from the victim's face, Phoebe gasped.

Virginia looked at her mother. "I can't tell, Mama," she said. "I don't know …"

Attending the inquest were Red Manley (front), Phoebe Short, Adrian West, and Virginia West (second row, from left).

Phoebe wasn't sure either. She told Hansen that Betty had a birthmark on her right shoulder. She'd be able to recognize that. The sheet was lowered more, and Phoebe saw the birthmark. It was Betty. Phoebe and Virginia burst into tears.

The detectives gave Phoebe and Virginia a few minutes to compose themselves. Then they took them to the coroner's hearing room at the Hall of Justice, where the inquest would take place. Coroner Ben H. Brown led the proceedings, which lasted 45 minutes and produced no real surprises. The witnesses called to testify in front of the nine inquest jurors were Detectives Harry Hansen and Jesse Haskins, Dr. Frederick Newbarr, Phoebe Short, and Red Manley. Based on the testimony, the jurors decided Betty's death was a homicide.

Two days later, on January 24, *Examiner* editor James Richardson got a disturbing phone call. The man on the other end of the line said he liked the way the newspaper had covered the Black Dahlia case. However, the man said, the paper seemed to have run out of new material to print. He added that perhaps he could help in that regard. The man offered to send the newspaper some of the belongings Betty had with her when she vanished.

Richardson grabbed a sheet of paper and frantically wrote, "Trace this call." He showed the note to his secretary, but the caller didn't stay on the line long enough for the call to be traced.

A small package, postmarked the day of the phone call, was redirected to the postal inspector's office because it was open on one end. The package was addressed to "Los Angeles *Examiner* and other papers." The inspector called the *Examiner*, and the next morning, the package was opened at the Federal Building. Several people involved in the case were there, including homicide detectives and reporters.

The package contained several items known to have been in Betty's purse when she disappeared. Among the items were her Social Security card, an address book, her birth certificate, and claim tickets for the luggage she had checked at the bus station

The package addressed to the *Examiner* contained items Betty was carrying when she disappeared.

January 9. There was also a note that had been made using letters cut from newspapers. It read: "Here is Dahlia's belongings—letter to follow."

Police examined the envelope but found only smudged fingerprints. No matches to the fingerprints were ever found.

Detectives noticed, however, that several names and addresses had been cut out of the address book that was in the envelope. Could the name of the killer be one of the missing entries?

The address book provided another lead. On the book's cover, the name "Mark Hansen" and "1937" were stamped in gold. Hansen ran the Florentine Gardens, a nightclub in Los Angeles where gangsters including Bugsy Siegel and Mickey Cohen liked to hang out. Betty had sometimes gone to the club as well. Along with several other young women, she also occasionally had stayed at Hansen's home, which was behind the club.

When questioned by police, Hansen denied having had a romantic relationship with Betty. He also said he'd never used the address book. It had been a gift to him, but it had disappeared from his home. Handwriting experts examined the entries and determined Betty had been the only person to write in the book.

Police released a public statement about the address book January 27: "A complete roundup of the 75 names in the Mark Hansen address book was completed yesterday without adding anything to the sorry story that is already known."

The same day, a postcard arrived by mail at the *Examiner*, as promised earlier by whoever sent the package containing the address book and Betty's other belongings. Police believed the postcard had been sent by the killer, the man who had called the newspaper just days earlier. The message on the postcard read:

Here it is
Turning in Wed
Jan. 29 10 A.M.
Had my fun at Police
Black Dahlia Avenger

Police believed the message meant the killer intended to turn himself in to authorities at 10:00 a.m. January 29.

"The fact that the postcard was printed rather than lettered with words cut out of newspapers also supports the theory that the killer intends to turn himself in to the police, and no longer needs to take pains to conceal his identity," said Captain Jack Donahoe, chief of homicide in the Los Angeles Police Department's Central Division.

Donahoe responded to the suspected killer through the newspapers.

"If you want to surrender as indicated by the postcard now in our hands, I will meet you at any public location at any time or at the Homicide detail office at City Hall," Donahoe said. The captain included a phone number where he could be reached. But if the suspect called, he probably got a busy signal. The phone line was overloaded with calls from people pretending to be the "Black Dahlia Avenger."

Donahoe still hoped the suspect would show up at the *Examiner* building at 10:00 a.m. January 29. An hour before the appointed time, detectives were posted at each of the building's doors. When the clock struck 10, no one showed up. The same thing happened the next hour and the next. Either the Black Dahlia Avenger had changed his mind, or he had never intended to come in the first place.

A GANGSTER NAMED BUGSY

Benjamin Siegel was one of the most vicious and most feared gangsters of the 1930s and 1940s. Fellow gang members nicknamed him "Bugsy" because they thought he was "crazy as a bedbug," as shown by his quick and violent temper. The son of poor Russian immigrants, Siegel grew up in Brooklyn, New York, and vowed to become rich and famous. Among his accomplishments was opening the flashy Flamingo Hotel in Las Vegas, Nevada, in 1946. The following year Siegel was gunned down as he read a newspaper in his girlfriend's Los Angeles home. His killer was never found.

CHAPTER 8

MANY SUSPECTS

As is often the case in high-profile crimes, police were bombarded with false confessions in the Black Dahlia case. Some who confessed wanted attention. Some just wanted a hot meal and a place to sleep—even if that meant a jail cell. Others were mentally ill.

Police received many tips from people who said they were witnesses. They believed they'd seen Betty between the time she'd left the Biltmore and the morning her body was found. Police also found the luggage that Betty had checked at the Los Angeles bus station January 9. Whether the suitcases yielded any clues isn't known, because the police never revealed their contents to the public.

More than 400 members of the Los Angeles Police Department and the county sheriff's department were assigned to the case. They followed up every lead, questioned residents of the Leimert Park neighborhood, interrogated sex offenders, and searched for the location where Betty was killed.

"No matter how questionable each lead appeared on the surface, we had to track it down, and in this case, each lead seemed to open into something else, and it went on and on, and none of them were giving a clue to the missing week, or to the murder itself," Detective Finis Brown said later.

The police did develop a long list of suspects. Among them were Betty's friends Red Manley and Mark Hansen.

Manley, who suffered from mental problems, had been discharged early from the Army. Military authorities thought the pressure of military discipline was too much for him to handle. Being interrogated in connection with Betty's murder was even more difficult for him.

Manley was cleared as a suspect, but his life was ruined by his involvement with Betty. His story was published in newspapers across the country. He lost his wife and his job. Manley spent the rest of his life in and out of mental institutions. He was a patient at the Patton State Hospital in San Bernardino, California, when he committed suicide in 1986.

Mark Hansen was quickly eliminated as a suspect when he was able to supply an alibi. It wasn't so easy for another suspect, Leslie Dillon.

In October 1948 the 28-year-old Dillon was working as a bellhop in Miami, Florida. He sent a letter to Paul de River, a psychiatric consultant for the Los Angeles Police Department. Dillon wrote that he'd been following the case because he had lived in Los Angeles at the time of Betty's murder. He said one of his friends, Jeff Connors, had met Betty once at a Hollywood club. Dillon told de River that Connors might be able to help with the investigation.

De River called Dillon several times and talked about the case. He shared information with Dillon that hadn't been made known to the public. De River then talked to Los Angeles Police Chief Clemence Horrall. Based on the information from de River, Horrall decided that Dillon was a suspect.

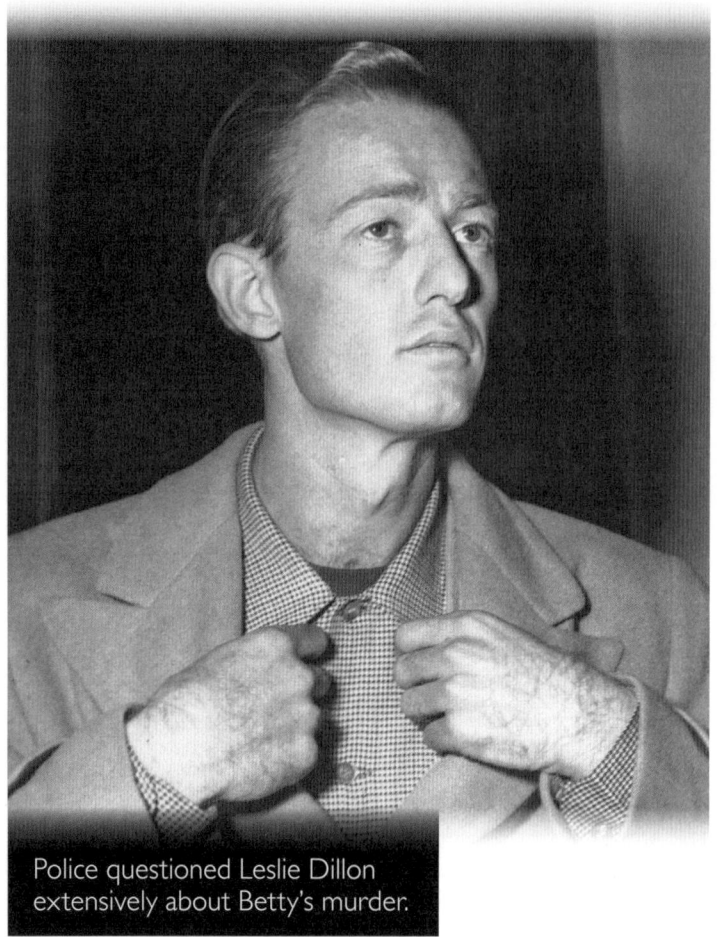

Police questioned Leslie Dillon extensively about Betty's murder.

He came up with a plan to get Dillon to come to California, and he asked for de River's help.

De River called Dillon and told him he was interested in hiring Dillon as his assistant at the LAPD. De River even hinted that he would be interested in working with Dillon on a book about the Black Dahlia investigation.

Reeling Dillon in, de River said he'd send the young man a plane ticket to Las Vegas, Nevada, and arrange for a place for him to stay. But when Dillon arrived at the Las Vegas airport January 10, 1949, de River met him with a limousine. Dillon accepted the ride to Los Angeles.

Along the way the two talked about the murder case. Dillon didn't know he was being taped by Lieutenant Willie Burns, who was driving the limo.

Dillon again told the story of how his friend Jeff Connors had met Betty. De River tried to twist Dillon's story, suggesting there was no friend. He hinted that when Dillon talked about "Jeff Connors," he might actually be talking about himself. Suddenly Dillon was being accused of being mentally unstable. Did he have something to feel guilty about? Was this why he had contacted de River about this horrific case? Had he killed Betty and locked the truth away in his mind where even he himself couldn't recall it?

In Banning, California, Burns drove into a motel parking lot. Dillon later said it was there that de River accused him of killing Betty. After Burns handcuffed him, Dillon was led to a motel room.

"They kept me in the motel room until three or four other men arrived, and then they began to question me," Dillon said. "In the middle of it, de River insisted I was 'too knowledgeable,' and 'too intelligent' to conceal the truth from myself. I said I didn't know what I'd be concealing from myself, and he said 'facts too painful to remember.' Then he began to ask me intimate details about the mutilations and the things that had been done to the Dahlia. But the only things I knew about them was

"DE RIVER WOULD ASK ME A QUESTION AND THEN PUT THE ANSWER RIGHT IN MY MOUTH."

what I'd read in the papers and from the detective magazine and what de River had told me. But de River would ask me a question and then put the answer right in my mouth."

The questioning continued when police officers drove Dillon to the Strand Hotel in Los Angeles. Dillon was told that police had been unable to find his friend Jeff Connors.

"[De River] wanted me to confess I'd killed the Dahlia, and I couldn't confess to it," Dillon said. "But they had me just about convinced I was crazy or something, and that maybe I did kill the Dahlia, and then just forgot about it."

After questioning Dillon for a week, police charged him with the murder of Betty Short. The police told reporters that the killer had been caught. While Dillon was being questioned, he wasn't allowed to contact his family or a lawyer. But he managed to drop a note out a window of the hotel. In the note he said he was being held in the hotel in connection with the Black Dahlia case, and he wanted a lawyer. He addressed the message to Los Angeles attorney Jerry Geisler.

Dillon finally had a stroke of luck. Someone discovered his note, and it found its way to Geisler. It didn't take long to prove that Dillon had nothing to do with Betty's death. Witnesses and employment records helped prove he had been in San Francisco, California, at the time of the murder. Geisler's investigators also found Jeff Connors, who confirmed the story that he had met Betty at a Hollywood bar.

IT SEEMED LIKELY THAT A DOCTOR WAS INVOLVED.

Police quietly dismissed Dillon as a suspect. In addition, de River was found to be a fraud. He wasn't a psychiatrist or even a doctor, and he resigned from the police department.

The police looked at other suspects as well. Even gangster Bugsy Siegel and Betty's father, Cleo, were considered. But no one was ever brought to trial.

Some investigators suspected that more than one person was responsible for the murder. It seemed likely that a doctor was involved. The cut that severed Betty's body was made with such precision that police thought a surgeon likely made it.

As months and then years dragged on without an arrest, the press and the public questioned the LAPD's handling of the case. In 1949 a Los Angeles grand jury examined the murder. The grand jurors found evidence of corrupt practices and other misconduct by some law enforcement officials involved in the case, as well as an "alarming" increase in unsolved murders. But the jury's findings didn't bring the case any closer to a conclusion.

CHAPTER 9

CONTINUED INTEREST

On January 26, 1947, Elizabeth Short was quietly buried at Mountain View Cemetery in Oakland, California. Just a few of her family members attended the ceremony. Police stood nearby just in case the killer decided to make an appearance.

A simple pink marble marker graces her gravesite. It says:

Daughter

Elizabeth Short

July 29, 1924 — Jan. 15, 1947

Betty was buried in a simple ceremony at Mountain View Cemetery in Oakland, California.

Though Betty's body was laid to rest, her story has continued to puzzle and fascinate people.

Detective Harry Hansen worked on the Black Dahlia case from January 15, 1947, until his retirement 23 years later. In a March 1971 newspaper interview, Hansen admitted that not solving the Black Dahlia case was the biggest disappointment of his career.

"Being objective didn't mean that we didn't want that killer. I never wanted anything more," he said. "Every now and then there'd be some new development, a lead would pop out of nowhere and we'd think, here it is, this is it! But it never really was."

At first police thought other murders would follow Betty's. They feared they had a serial killer on their hands.

"You had the importance of immediate action," said one investigator. "All off-duty officers were called in, and known sex offenders were being picked up, interviewed—alibis established, checked and rechecked."

As time went by, though, it didn't seem likely that a serial killer had murdered Betty. There were other unsolved murders of young women in the city around that time, but none seemed to match the pattern of Betty's death.

As time has passed and suspects have been questioned and dismissed, the Elizabeth Short murder investigation has grown cold. Yet Hollywood has kept the Black Dahlia case in the public eye. A 1975 TV movie called *Who Is the Black Dahlia?* starred Efrem Zimbalist Jr. as Harry Hansen and Lucie Arnaz as Elizabeth Short. A 2006 movie called *The Black Dahlia* was directed by Brian De Palma and had an all-star cast, including Josh Harnett, Aaron Eckhart, Hilary Swank, and Scarlett Johansson. Mia Kirshner played Elizabeth Short. The film earned several award nominations.

Many books and Internet sites also are devoted to keeping the memory of the Black Dahlia alive. James

IN DEATH BETTY ACHIEVED THE FAME SHE DESIRED MOST OF HER LIFE.

Ellroy fictionalized the murder case in his 1987 novel *The Black Dahlia*. In 2003 a book by Steve Hodel, *The Black Dahlia Avenger*, claimed to solve the mystery. Hodel said he believes his father, George Hodel, killed Elizabeth Short, but police found many holes in his theory. Among them are images in George Hodel's photo album that Steve Hodel claims are of Betty. To the untrained eye, the photos don't look much like Betty. A professional photo identification expert hired in 2004 by the CBS TV network also concluded that Elizabeth Short is not the woman shown in the photos.

Because Betty's murder occurred so long ago, her killer is probably dead as well. But as long as the

Steve Hodel claimed that photos taken by his father were of Betty Short.

memory of her life and death remains, solving this terrible crime may still be possible.

In death Betty achieved the fame she desired most of her life. Though most people don't remember the name Elizabeth Short, her nickname—the Black Dahlia—remains familiar to many even now, more than six decades after her murder.

TIMELINE

July 29
1924 — Elizabeth "Betty" Short is born in Hyde Park, Massachusetts.

1940 — Betty moves to Miami Beach, Florida, for the winter. She later drops out of high school.

December
1942 — Betty moves in with her father in Vallejo, California.

August
1944 — Betty moves to Los Angeles, California.

December 6
1946
Betty travels to San Diego, California, and stays with Elvera French and her family. In San Diego she begins dating Robert "Red" Manley.

January 8
1947
Betty leaves the Frenches' house with Manley.

January 9
1947
Betty walks out of the Biltmore Hotel in Los Angeles, California, about 10:00 p.m. It is the last time she is seen alive.

January 15
1947
Betty's mutilated body is found in an empty lot in the Leimert Park area of Los Angeles.

TIMELINE

January 19 1947 — Police arrest Robert Manley and question him about Betty's death; they release him two days later.

January 22 1947 — A coroner's jury rules Betty's death to be a homicide.

January 24 1947 — *Los Angeles Examiner* editor James Richardson gets a phone call from a man who claims to have some of the belongings Betty had with her when she disappeared.

January 25 1947 — A package containing Betty's birth certificate, Social Security card, bus terminal claim tickets, and address book is opened at the Los Angeles postal inspector's office.

January 26
1947
Betty is buried in a cemetery in Oakland, California.

January 10
1949
Police arrest Leslie Dillon as a suspect in Betty's murder and question him for a week; he is later released.

2006
A movie about the case, *The Black Dahlia*, is released.

GLOSSARY

alibi—evidence that a person accused of a crime was somewhere else when the crime was committed

autopsy—an examination performed on a dead body to find the cause of death

civilian—a person who is not in the military

coroner—a medical official who investigates unexpected or unnatural deaths

dahlia—a type of flower

gurney—a cot or stretcher with wheels

heinous—awful

homicide—the willful killing of one person by another person

inquest—an official inquiry into a crime, often conducted by a judge or coroner

intimate—very personal

intriguing—quite interesting

mug shot—a police photograph of an arrested person

mutilated—cut up

precision—accuracy

scoop—information of immediate interest

sophisticated—experienced in the ways of the world

ADDITIONAL RESOURCES

READ MORE

Editors of *Life* magazine. *Life: Greatest Unsolved Mysteries of All Time*. New York: Life Books, 2009.

Editors of *Life* magazine. *The Most Notorious Crimes in American History*. New York: Life Books, 2007.

Newton, Michael. *The Encyclopedia of Unsolved Crimes*. New York: Facts on File, 2009.

Schechter, Harold, ed. *True Crime: An American Anthology*. New York: Library of America, 2008.

INTERNET SITES

Use FactHound to find Internet sites related to this book. All of the sites on FactHound have been researched by our staff.

Here's all you do:
Visit *www.facthound.com*
Type in this code: 9780756543587

SELECT BIBLIOGRAPHY

Black Dahlia—News. 23 March 2010. http://blackdahlia.info/modules/news/article.php?storyid=1

The Black Dahlia Story: The Unsolved Murder of Elizabeth Short. 23 March 2010. www.trutv.com/library/crime/notorious_murders/famous/dahlia/index_1.html

Federal Bureau of Investigation. Elizabeth Ann Short. 23 March 2010. http://foia.fbi.gov/foiaindex/short_e.htm

Gilmore, John. *Severed: The True Story of the Black Dahlia Murder.* Los Angeles: Zanja Press, 1994.

Hodel, Steve. *Black Dahlia Avenger: A Genius for Murder.* New York: Arcade Publishing, 2003.

Secrets of the Dead. 23 March 2010. www.pbs.org/wnet/
secrets/executed-in-error/perennial-thrillers-murder-
mystery-obsession

Top 25 Crimes of the Century—The Black Dahlia. *Time*.
23 March 2010. www.time.com/time/2007/crimes/5.html

Wolfe, Donald H. *The Black Dahlia Files: The Mob, the
Mogul, and the Murder That Transfixed Los Angeles*.
New York: ReganBooks, 2005.

INDEX

Bauerdorf, Georgette, 32
Bersinger, Betty, 49–50, 51, 52
B-girls, 31
Biltmore Hotel, 45, 47, 61, 73
Brown, Finis, 52, 61, 63, 74

Camp Cooke, 25–26, 55
Clement, Maurice, 38–39
Connors, Jeff, 75, 77, 79, 80
crime scene, 49–50, 51, 52–53

de River, Paul, 75, 76–77, 78, 79, 80
Dillon, Leslie, 75–80
Donahoe, Jack, 70, 71

evidence, 53, 58, 66–70, 73

false confessions, 70, 73
Federal Bureau of Investigation (FBI), 54–55
Fickling, Joseph, 33, 34–35, 37
fingerprints, 27, 54–55, 57, 68
Fowler, Will, 56, 59, 63
French, Dorothy, 41, 43, 44, 58–59
French, Elvera, 41, 43, 58–59

Gordon, Matt, 33–34, 41, 43

Hansen, Harry, 52, 53, 57, 61, 63, 65, 84, 85
Hansen, Mark, 68, 69, 74, 75
Hodel, George, 86
Hodel, Steve, 86
Hollywood Canteen, 32–33

inquest, 12, 63, 65

Leimert Park neighborhood, 11, 49, 73
Los Angeles Examiner (newspaper), 9, 12, 54, 55–56, 59, 63, 65–66, 69, 71
Los Angeles Herald-Express (newspaper), 53, 56

Manley, Robert "Red," 11, 12, 44–45, 47, 59, 61, 63, 65, 74–75
movies, 18–19, 23, 32, 35, 36, 41, 85

Newbarr, Frederick, 57–58, 65

Richardson, James, 9, 11, 12, 56, 59, 65, 66

Short, Cleo, 15–16, 18, 20–21, 23, 25, 29, 81
Short, Elizabeth "Betty"
 arrest of, 27, 55
 autopsy of, 57–58
 birth of, 15
 burial of, 83
 childhood of, 15–16, 18–19
 health problems of, 19–20
 identification of, 53–55, 63, 65
 murder of, 11–12, 52–54, 58
 nickname of, 35, 57, 87
 travels of, 15, 20, 23, 25, 31, 33, 35, 37–38, 39, 45
Short, Muriel, 15, 18–19
Short, Phoebe, 9, 11–12, 15, 18, 19, 20–21, 29, 33, 44, 63, 65
Short, Virginia, 15, 39, 45, 47, 63, 65
Siegel, Benjamin "Bugsy," 68, 71, 81
Soundphoto machines, 54
suspects, 12, 32, 58, 59, 61, 69–71, 74–81, 85, 86
Sutton, Wain, 9, 11, 12, 44

Underwood, Aggie, 53, 56

witnesses, 65, 73, 80

ABOUT THE AUTHOR

Brenda Haugen started in the newspaper business and had a career as an award-winning journalist before finding her niche as an author. Since then, she has written and edited many books, most of them for children. A graduate of the University of North Dakota in Grand Forks, Brenda lives in North Dakota with her family.